12-Bar Blues Guitar Licks

by Dave Rubin

Audio Access Included!

The book is dedicated to the memory of Smokin' Joe Kubek.

PLAYBACK+
Speed • Pitch • Balance • Loop

To access audio, visit:
www.halleonard.com/mylibrary

Enter Code
1882-7136-2039-7971

ISBN 978-1-70514-165-6

HAL•LEONARD®

Visit Hal Leonard Online at
www.halleonard.com

World headquarters, contact:
Hal Leonard
7777 West Bluemound Road
Milwaukee, WI 53213
Email: info@halleonard.com

In Europe, contact:
Hal Leonard Europe Limited
1 Red Place
London, W1K 6PL
Email: info@halleonardeurope.com

In Australia, contact:
Hal Leonard Australia Pty. Ltd.
4 Lentara Court
Cheltenham, Victoria, 3192 Australia
Email: info@halleonard.com.au

About the Author

Dave Rubin is a New York City blues guitarist, teacher, author, and journalist. He has played with Son Seals, Honeyboy Edwards, Steady Rollin' Bob Margolin, Billy Boy Arnold, Johnny Copeland, Chuck Berry, James Brown's JBs, the Drifters, Marvelettes, Coasters, and the Campbell Brothers. In addition, he has performed on the Blues Alley TV show in Philadelphia and New York Now in the city and has made commercials for Mountain Dew and the Oreck company.

Dave has been an author for Hal Leonard for over 30 years, writing books in series such as Inside the Blues, Signature Licks, Guitar School, Play Like, and other assorted titles. He was the musical director for the Star Licks DVD series Legends of the Blues, as well as being featured in the 12-Bar Blues accompanying video for his book that was nominated for a Paul Revere Award in 1999.

As a journalist, Dave has written for *Guitar Player*, *Guitar World*, *Guitar One*, *Living Blues*, *Guitar Shop*, and *Blues Access* magazines. Dave was the recipient of the 2005 Keeping the Blues Alive award in journalism from the Blues Foundation in Memphis, Tennessee.

About the Audio

All of the musical figures within this book are demonstrated with audio recordings so that you can more easily master the language of these blues masters. Just go to **www.halleonard.com/mylibrary** and input the code found on page 1 of this book.

Introduction

Akin to Zeus hurling thunderbolts to earth, the mighty Gibson company introduced the first commercially viable electric guitar in 1936 with the ES-150. The guitar world would never be the same. Despite the "ES" prefix for "Electric Spanish," it bore no resemblance to a classical or flattop acoustic, but instead was a thinline acoustic archtop design beloved by jazz guitarists. Indeed, the legendary Charlie Christian became so known for playing one (and the more deluxe ES-250) that it eventually became known as the "Charlie Christian model."

Think of this book as a compendium of curated electric blues guitar licks from some of the greatest postwar artists. They are arranged by decade from the 1940s to the 1980s, featuring the players in roughly chronological order. I focus on five short examples from each, which nail their iconic style while also making them accessible. Learn them and a broad spectrum of improvisational concepts will be literally at your fingertips.

Observe how they evolve over time from jazzy eighth-note lines to faster, aggressively swinging manipulated bent-note clusters of hammer-ons and pull-offs. In addition, with exceptions, I have chosen to present licks drawn from I–IV chord changes typically found in measures 1 and 2 of the "fast change" 12-bar blues. As those changes appear the most and by their nature elicit the most powerful forward musical motion, their importance cannot be exaggerated. As Who drummer Keith Moon once remarked regarding solos, " Everyone just remembers your entrance and exit. The rest is forgotten." While obviously an overstatement and possibly even tongue-in-cheek given the source, his point bears scrutiny.

I hope you gain as much and enjoy the licks as much as I did putting them to paper. To use one of my favorite quotes from Peter Green-era Fleetwood Mac: "Then Play On" (with apologies to that creative picker of words, William Shakespeare).

Dave Rubin, NYC, 2021

Contents

Chapter I: 1940s

Aaron Thibeaux "T-Bone" Walker
(1910–1975)

T-Bone Walker is the "Father of Electric Blues Guitar," while his friend/counterpart, Charlie Christian, is the "Father of Electric Jazz Guitar." With the single-string soloing influences of Blind Lemon Jefferson and Lonnie Johnson, combined with his impeccable rhythm derived at least in part from his dancing ability, he forged the template for virtually every blues guitarist who followed in his gracefully swinging swath.

Performance Tip: The composite blues scale afforded him both jazzy melodies and down-home blues funk.

Fig. 1

*To access this audio and others throughout the book, just go to **www.halleonard.com/mylibrary** and input the code found on page 1!*

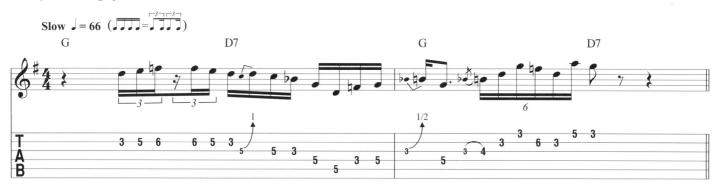

Fig. 2

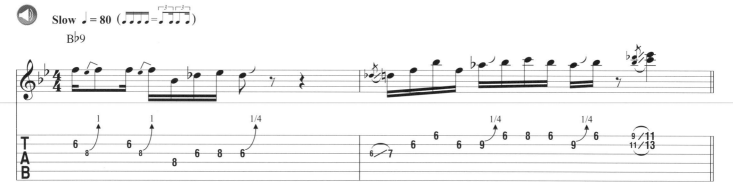

Fig. 3

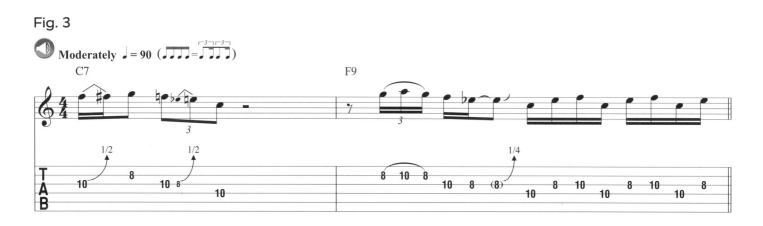

Fig. 4

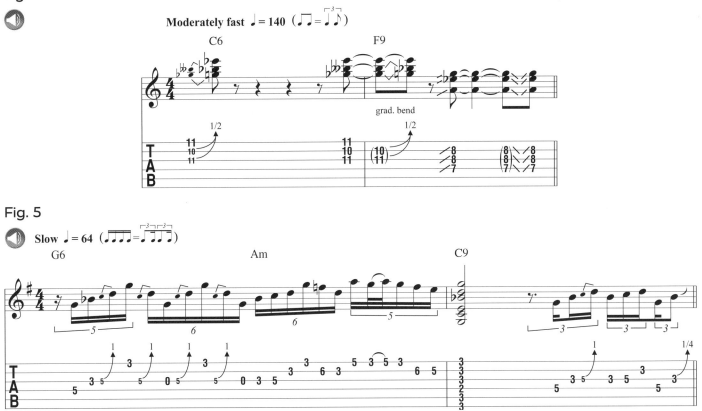

Fig. 5

Johnny Moore
(1906–1969)

Best known with his Three Blazers as the backing band for blues singer Charles Brown in the 1940s, Johnny Moore delivered the jazzier side of blues and nascent rhythm 'n' blues. In addition, he set a precedent for the many who followed down to Kenny Burrell and beyond. Clean, rich tone and suave phrasing while gracefully navigating chord changes proved him a sensitive accompanist who soloed "inside" the song.

Performance Tip: Strong chord tones and arpeggios stand out in his playing.

Fig. 6

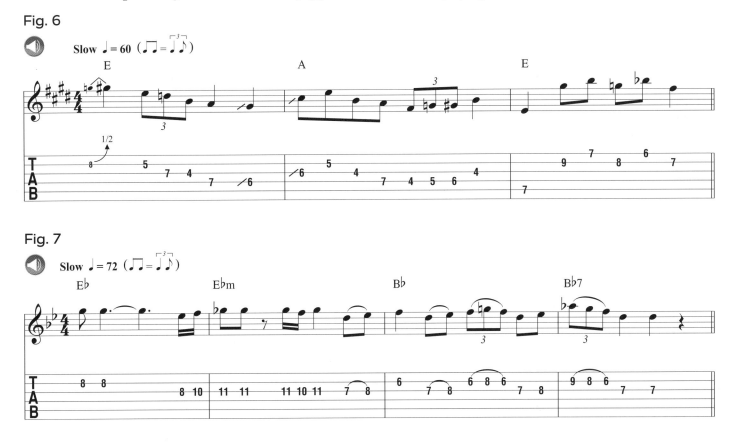

Fig. 7

Fig. 8

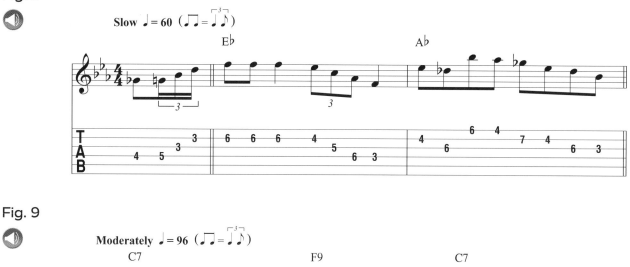

Fig. 9

Fig. 10

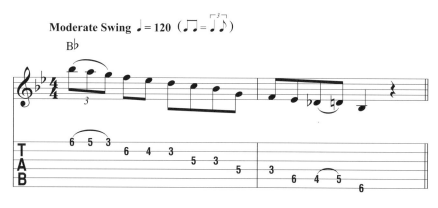

Oscar Moore
(1916–1981)

The brother of Johnny Moore, Oscar made musical history with the Nat King Cole Trio, itself the progenitor of the groups of Charles Brown and early Ray Charles. Dynamic, whether flexing his chops or laying back when appropriate, his lines flow like aged-in-wood bourbon.

Performance Tip: Contributing to his seamlessly composed licks is his regular employment of "blues boxes."

Fig. 11

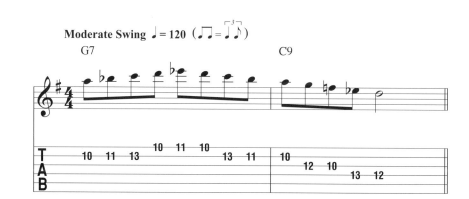

Fig. 12

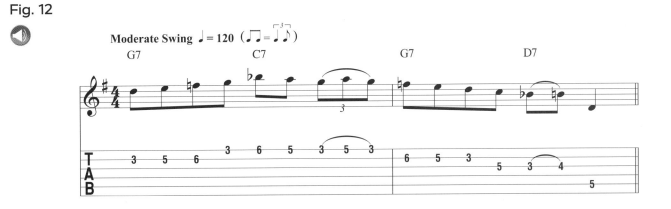

Fig. 13

Fig. 14

Fig. 15

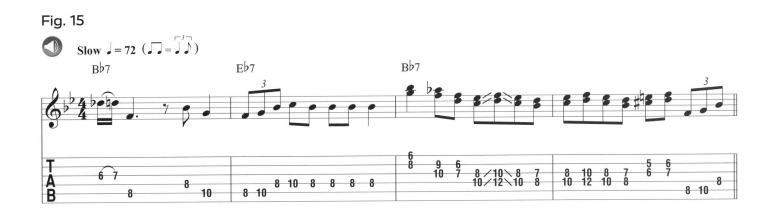

Carl Hogan
(1917–1977)

To only reference Carl Hogan as having had a profound influence on Chuck Berry (see "Ain't That Just Like a Woman") is to deny his significant contribution to blues guitar with Louis Jordan. Like the Yardbirds and the Bluesbreakers in the 1960s, Jordan had a succession of three exceptional guitarists with Hogan leading off the musical parade.

Performance Tip: As would be expected from a guitarist backing the famous "Shuffle King," his licks locked into the groove like the gears on a 1945 Cadillac Coupe de Ville.

Fig. 16

Fig. 17

Fig. 18

Fig. 19

Fig. 20

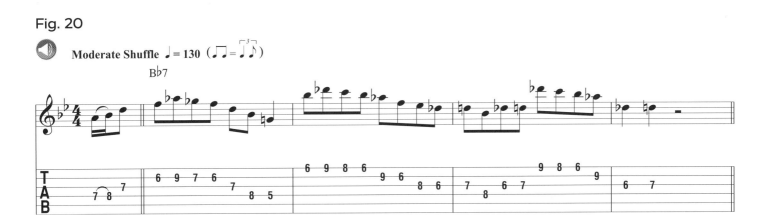

Roosevelt James "Ham" Jackson
(Dates Unknown)

In relative chronological order, the second great blues guitarist in the "string" of Louis Jordan ace sidemen. Unfortunately, very little biographical info is available about Jackson, but his playing speaks clearly for his renown.

Performance Tip: Rhythmic drive and dynamic musical tension through repetition are cornerstones of his style.

Fig. 21

Fig. 22

Fig. 23

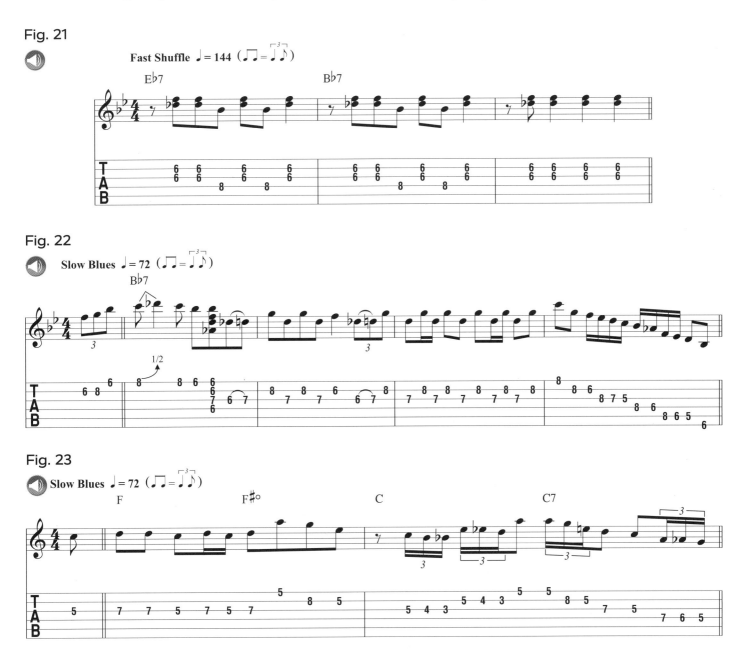

Fig. 24

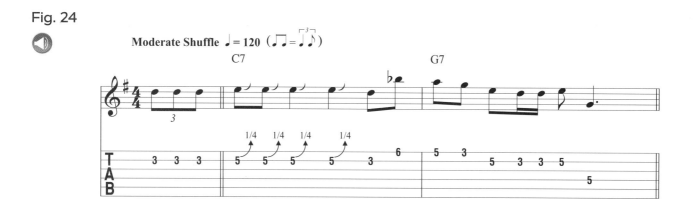

Fig. 25

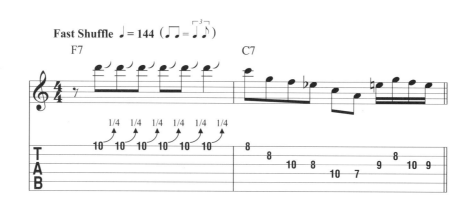

Chapter II: 1950s

Clarence "Gatemouth" Brown
(1924–2005)

Like his contemporary and frequent "dueling blues guitar" competition T-Bone Walker, Gatemouth Brown is a legend of postwar Texas blues. Besides being a virtuoso six-string picker, he also excelled on violin, harmonica, mandolin, and drums. He is acknowledged as the first to lead a big band with loud electric guitar, and his breadth of musical knowledge extended to jazz, Cajun, country, and even proto-rock 'n' roll. His instrumentals, topped by "Okey-Dokey Stomp" and various boogie woogie rave-ups, are essential blues guitar tutorials.

Performance Tip: No plectrum for him, Brown used his thumb and index fingers along with a capo. Power and finesse built upon muscular technique are hallmarks of his music.

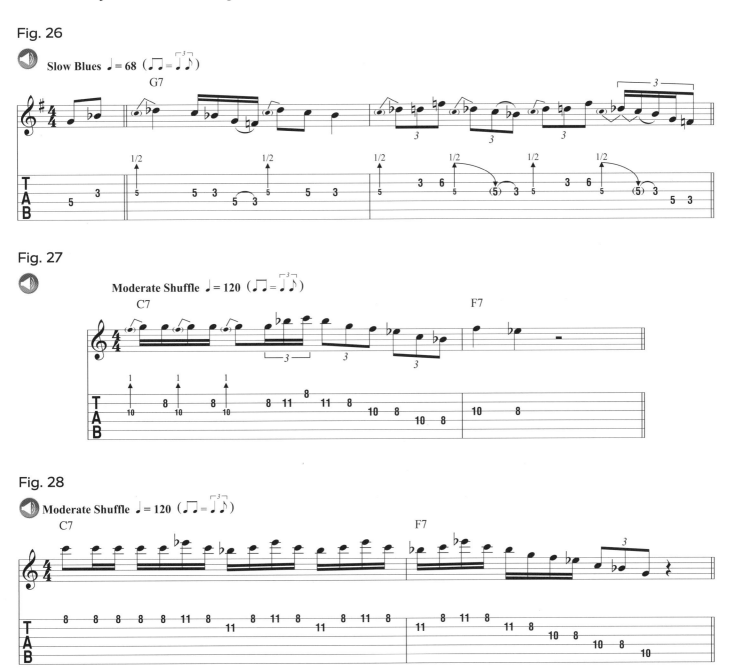

Fig. 26

Fig. 27

Fig. 28

Fig. 29

Fig. 30

Eddie "Guitar Slim" Jones
(1926–1959)

One of the all-time characters in the blues was a legend in his own time of the 1950s. He would dye his hair blue and stroll out into the audience with a 100-foot cable while living the prototypical "rock star" lifestyle of wine and women. Of more lasting importance, however, was his overdriven tone and heartrending emotional playing and singing.

Performance Tip: Like Johnny "Guitar" Watson, Jones was one of the few postwar electric blues guitarists to not overtly exhibit the pervasive influence of B.B. King. Contributing significantly to his idiosyncratic style was his prominent use of the major pentatonic scale, as well as his staccato phrasing.

Fig. 31

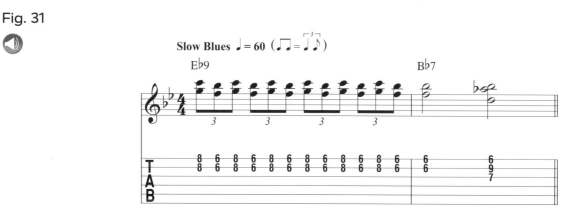

Fig. 32

Fig. 33

Fig. 34

Fig. 35

Bill Jennings
(1919–1978)

Sometimes called the "Architect of Soul-Jazz" in reference to his later tenure with Willis "Gator Tail" Jackson, Brother Jack McDuff, and others, Bill Jennings is a verifiable, if "unsung," blues guitar hero. He is third in line from the lauded trio of Louis Jordan guitarists to contribute hot and cool licks to the leader's jive-shuffling, classic legacy. In addition, he continued playing on through the '50s, '60s, and '70s as a leader and valued sideman.

Performance Tip: Be aware Jennings was left-handed and played right-handed guitars upside down à la Albert King and Otis Rush (but not Jimi Hendrix), resulting in vigorous string bending. That said, like other jazzy blues guitarists of the era and beyond, he often favored the composite blues scale, a combination of the blues scale and Mixolydian mode.

Fig. 36

Fig. 37

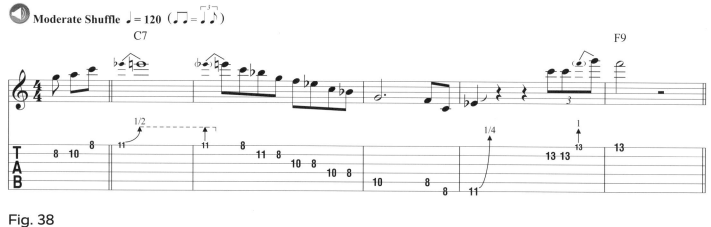

Fig. 38

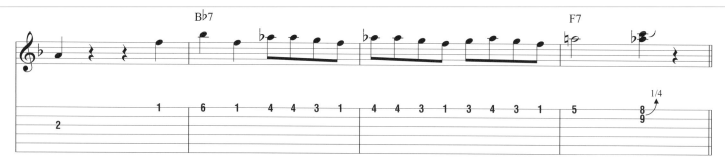

Fig. 39

Fig. 40

Johnny "Guitar" Watson
(1935–1996)

"Young John Watson" took his appropriate nickname from a Joan Crawford movie in 1954. The same year, he recorded the groundbreaking "Space Guitar," utilizing unusually heavy reverb to dramatically enhance his ferocious blues riffing. Preceding Jimi Hendrix by more than ten years, he made his guitar talk, grunt, and howl exuberantly. By the 1970s, he had transformed his sartorial style and music to funky soul and R&B. Following the shooting of his former notorious running buddy rock 'n' roll pioneer Larry Williams in 1980, he made significant life changes, however, and enjoyed a productive career into the 1990s.

Performance Tip: Watson eschewed the use of a pick, preferring his thumb and index fingers instead. Like Gatemouth Brown, Albert Collins, and others (including Jimmy Vaughan), he also employed a capo.

Fig. 41

Fig. 42

B.B. King
(1925–2015)

Like his main influence T-Bone Walker, B.B. King essentially influenced nearly every blues (and rock) guitarist who followed in his path. Possessed of "big ears," he also absorbed the music of Johnny Moore, Charlie Christian, and even Django Reinhardt. Though he would have never referred to himself as the "King of the Blues," a strong argument could be made for his ongoing benevolent reign as the "King of Postwar Electric Blues Guitar."

Performance Tip: B.B. was one of the most skilled and influential in "bending" the composite blues scale to his wishes. Combined with his slinky vibrato, it makes for the benchmark of expressive electric blues guitar soloing.

Performance Tip: One of the hallmarks of his style is the vigorous vibrato-ing of a note with his index finger. Be aware that he removes his thumb from the back of the neck in order to use his wrist to drive his hand and finger.

Fig. 46

Fig. 47

Fig. 48

Fig. 49

Fig. 50

Ike Turner
(1931–2007)

Ike Turner told this writer in an interview that he did not consider himself a guitar player, but a keyboardist instead. Going "hand-in-hand" with the statement was his admittance that he utilized the whammy bar on his Strat to not only execute rapid vibrato, but to bend strings as well— revolutionary for the early 1950s! His reasoning: "I thought that was how it was supposed to be done." A listen to his tracks with the Kings of Rhythm from the era confirms, besides being a legendary bandleader, songwriter, producer, and talent scout, Turner was very much a guitar player and a blues guitar hero at that.

Performance Tip: He tends to downpick most notes with few hammer-ons or pull-offs, resulting in an aggressive style bordering on violent.

Fig. 54

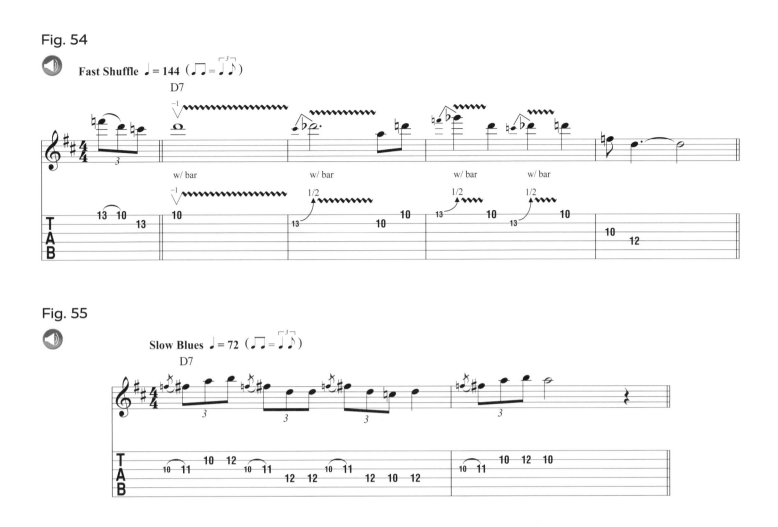

Otis Rush
(1934–2018)

The classic Cobra recordings of Otis Rush from the late 1950s, such as "I Can't Quit You, Baby," "All Your Love (I Miss Loving)," "My Love Will Never Die," and "Double Trouble," among others, came to define the Westside of Chicago sound as did those of Magic Sam and Buddy Guy. Somewhat as a detriment to his subsequent recording career, but not his rock solid reputation, was his reluctance to write new material.

Performance Tip: Playing left-handed and upside down contributed to his swooping, vocal-like bending and vibrato as he pulled down on the strings, as opposed to pushing up as most conventional players execute. Consequently, he tended to favor strings 1, 2, and 3 for their ease of accessibility.

Fig. 56

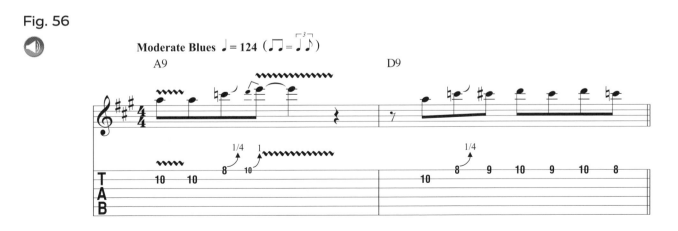

Fig. 57

Fast Blues ♩ = 152

Fig. 58

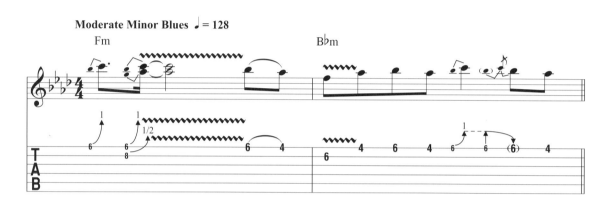

Moderate Minor Blues ♩ = 128

Fig. 59

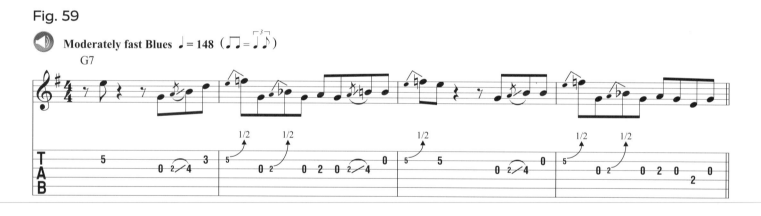

Moderately fast Blues ♩ = 148

Fig. 60

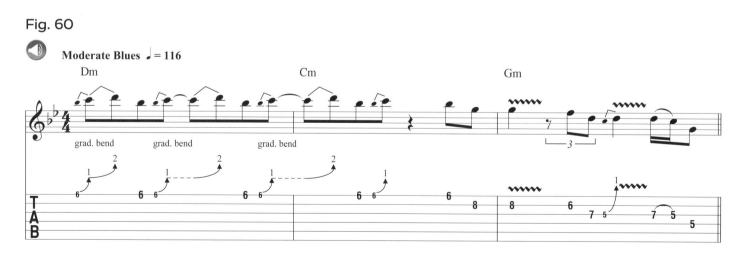

Moderate Blues ♩ = 116

Chapter III: 1960s

Albert Collins
(1932–1993)

"The Iceman" cometh, preceded by the piercing cry of a squeezed Telecaster. A Texas blues guitar legend who released his debut instrumental "Freeze" in 1958, Albert Collins left his first indelible mark on the blues with his signature instrumental "Frosty" in 1964, despite being an excellent singer. After stops and starts along the way, he found a welcoming and nurturing musical home in Chicago when he signed with Alligator Records in 1978, resulting in arguably his best work. An engaging and charismatic performer, he appeared at Live Aid with George Thorogood and the Destroyers in 1985 and in the movie *Adventures in Babysitting* in 1987.

Performance Tip: Collins tuned to open Fm, invariably employing a capo to afford him "open" strings in all keys and picking with his bare index finger and thumb. Note: The examples are transcribed in open Em for ease of accessibility.

21

Fig. 64

Em tuning:
(low to high) E-B-E-G-B-E

Fast Shuffle ♩ = 200

Fig. 65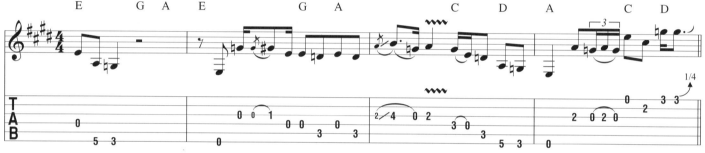

Em tuning:
(low to high) E-B-E-G-B-E

Moderate Rock ♩ = 132

Magic Sam
(1937–1969)

Sam "Magic Sam" Maghett is regarded by many as the greatest Chicago blues guitarist. Like his fellow Westside-of-Chicago firebrands Otis Rush and Buddy Guy, he recorded landmark blues guitar tracks for Cobra Records in the late 1950s, including "All Your Love," "Love Me with a Feeling," "Easy Baby," and others, with many in minor keys. An impassioned, soulful singer, he was also known for his instrumentals "I Feel So Good (I Wanna Boogie)" and "Lookin' Good." A productive move to Delmark Records in 1967 produced two classic albums. Tragically, he died young shortly after making a notable breakthrough performance at the Ann Arbor Blues Festival in 1969.

Performance Tip: Like Albert Collins and others, he eschewed picks in favor of using his thumb and index finger.

Fig. 66

Moderate Shuffle ♩ = 78

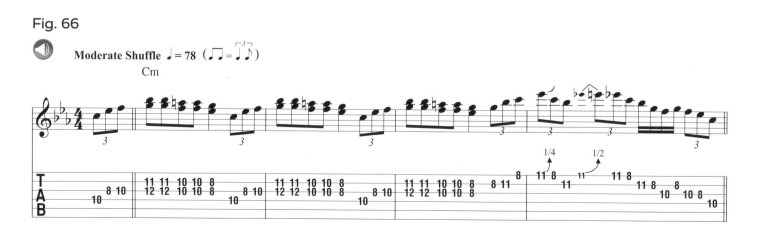

Fig. 67

 Moderate Shuffle ♩ = 116 (♪♪ = ³♪♪)

Fig. 68

Slow Blues ♩ = 80 (♪♪ = ³♪♪)

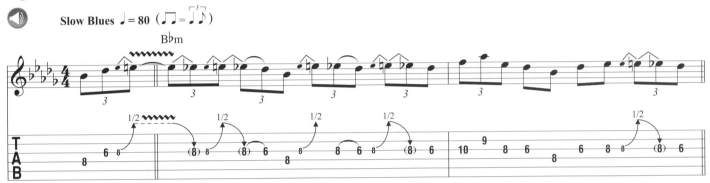

Fig. 69

Moderate Shuffle ♩ = 132 (♪♪ = ³♪♪)

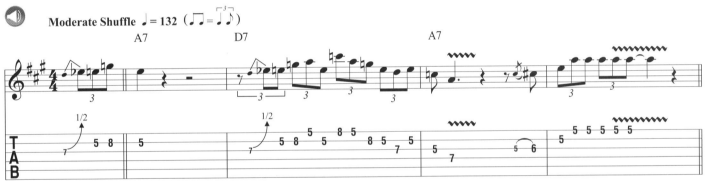

Fig. 70

Slow Blues ♩ = 72 (♪♪ = ³♪♪)

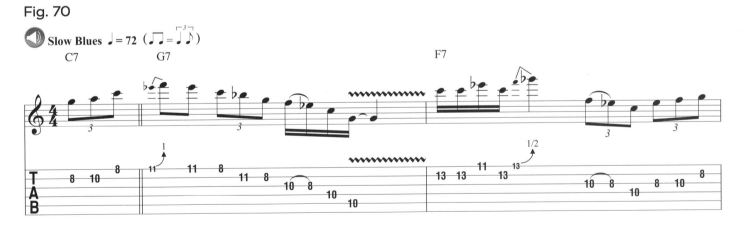

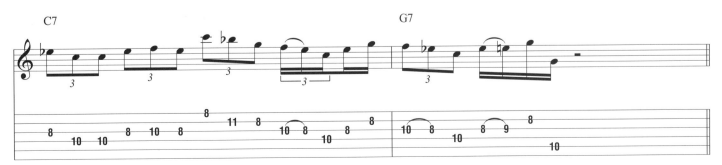

Billy Butler
(1924–1991)

One of the greatest postwar jazzy electric blues guitarists. His playing with Hammond B-3 organist Bill Doggett in the late 1950s and early 1960s is revered among guitarists, most notably on the instrumental guitar classic "Honky Tonk (Pts 1 & 2)" from 1956. Besides his solo recordings in the late 1960s and into the 1970s, he was a sideman on innumarble jazz, blues, R&B and funk sessions. In addition, he played the tasty solo on the mega-hit "Peppermint Twist" with Joey Dee & the Starlighters from 1961.

Performance Tip: Even when playing straight blues scale or minor pentatonic licks, Butler executes them with exquisite logic relative to the changes.

Fig. 71

Fig. 72

Fig. 73

Fig. 74

Fig. 75

Albert King
(1923–1992)

Albert King was king of the string-benders. In the early 1950s, he played drums with Jimmy Reed for a spell, but he recorded his first single singing and playing guitar to no acclaim. However, "Don't Throw Your Love on Me So Strong" in 1961 became an R&B hit, though subsequent releases failed to chart. Discouraged with scuffling in the St. Louis area, he relocated to Memphis in 1966, signing with Stax Records. It was the major turning point of his career as the soul and funk influences he absorbed added to his pugnacious blues with the landmark *Born Under a Bad Sign* in 1967 becoming a classic. Additionally, he found a new crossover audience who frequented the Fillmore West. When Stax went under in 1975, he moved from label to label with infrequent success over the succeeding years, though *In Session* with his "protégé" Stevie Ray Vaughan was a highlight for both.

Performance Tip: King was left-handed and played right-handed guitars upside down with light gauge strings, allowing for wide-interval bends as he pulled down like Otis Rush. Significantly, he employed a seeming variety of dropped tunings, including (low to high) B, E, B, E, G♯, and C♯, as used in the book *The Very Best of Albert King*. However, for instructional purposes, the examples are in standard tuning, as strings 3–1 in his open tuning are relative to standard.

Fig. 76

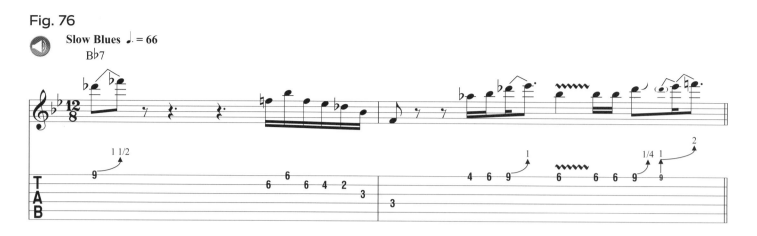

Fig. 77

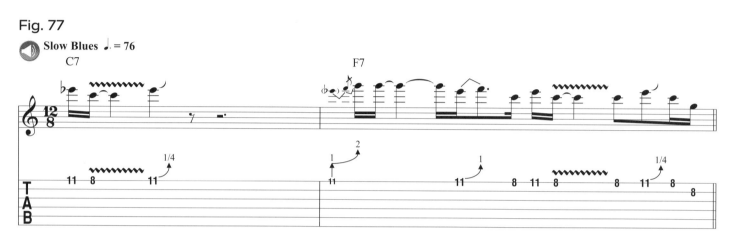

Fig. 78

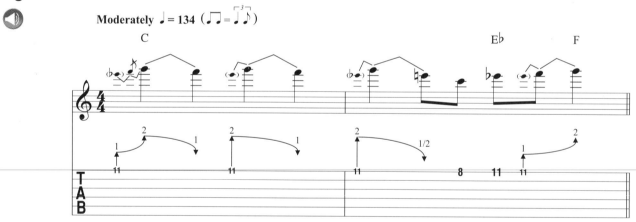

Fig. 79

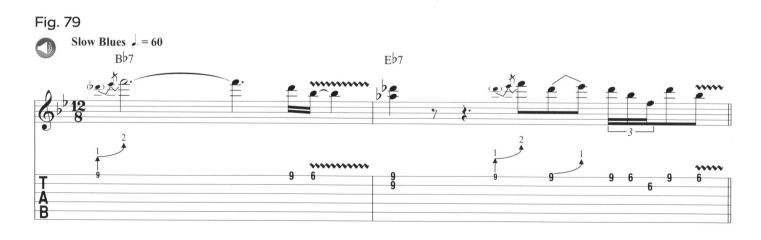

Fig. 80

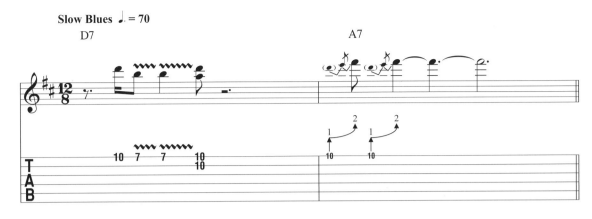

Freddie King
(1934–1976)

Freddie King is considered the "King of Guitar Kings" with his singing, playing, and songwriting. A "triple-threat" and a master of instrumental blues, it is virtually a rite of passage for blues guitarists to learn "Hide Away," and then if they are hooked, "The Stumble," "San Ho-Zay," "Remington Ride," and others. Though a son of the Lone Star State, where instrumentals were always popular, he recorded his classics at King Records in Cincinnatti and also spent time in Chicago.

Performance Tip: The "Texas Cannonball" used a plastic thumbpick and a metal index fingerpick, courtesy of advice from Jimmy Rogers when he relocated to Chicago in the '50s. The former was mainly reserved for bass-string riffs, but the latter was used for virtually all single-note lines and imparted a sharp attack with upstrokes in relation to pickup selection and amp EQ. However, a medium to heavy flatpick with appropriate guitar and amp settings can accomplish the same results.

Fig. 81

Fig. 82

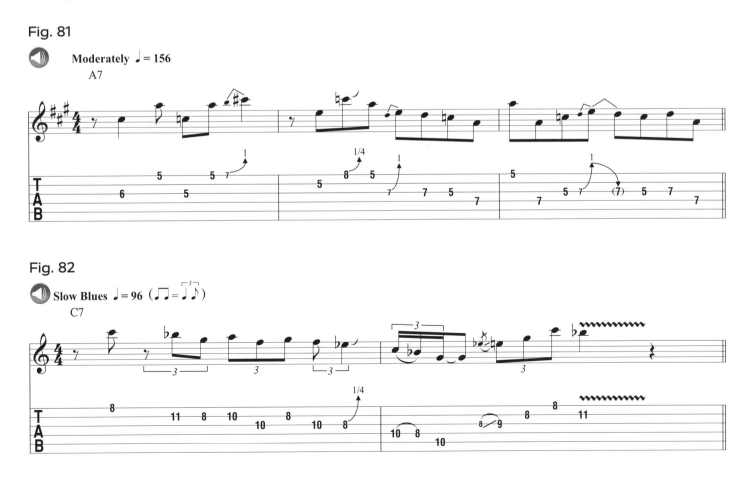

Fig. 83

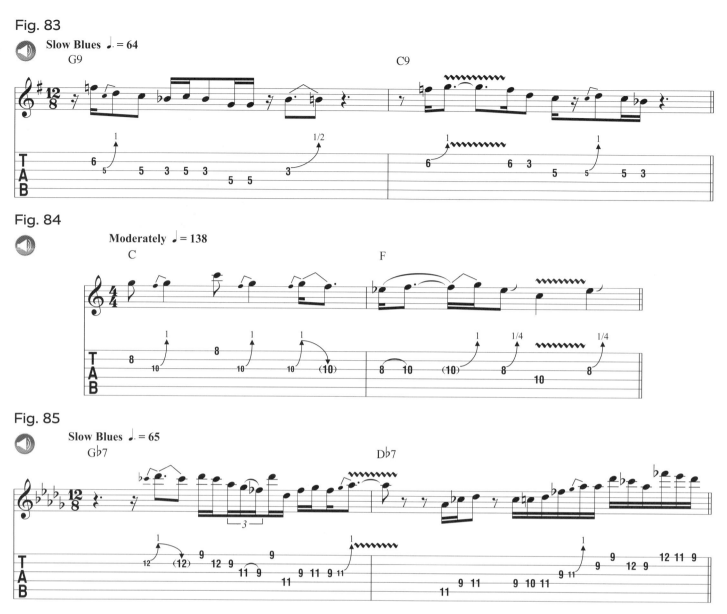

Fig. 84

Fig. 85

Hubert Sumlin
(1931–2011)

Chicago blues guitar hero Hubert Sumlin was a sweet man associated with literally a giant of the blues who was not so sweet to him. Either because or in spite of their relationship, Sumlin created tough licks and aggressive solos that always complimented Howlin' Wolf and his song. Any sampling would have to include "I Ain't Superstitious," "Three Hundred Pounds of Joy," "Built for Comfort," "Evil," "Louise," and "Killin' Floor." When Wolf died in 1976, Sumlin went through a long period of adjustment from sideman extraordinaire to esteemed solo artist in his own right.

Performance Tip: Like Freddie King, Hubert Sumlin picked with his thumb and index fingers but sans picks. It is highly recommended to try this technique, even if one ultimately opts to use picks. The warmer, fatter natural tone and feel can be quite inspiring.

Fig. 86

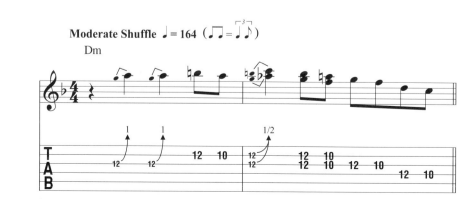

Buddy Guy
(1936–)

No less a fellow luminary, Eric Clapton called Buddy Guy "the best guitar player alive," for which an argument could be made. Unfortunately, he is the last of his generation, having outlived his fellow Westsiders Otis Rush and Magic Sam. His utter abandon and fearless improvising has inspired many, including Jimi Hendrix and Stevie Ray Vaughan. An anecdote told by Buddy to this writer: In the early '60s, he desired to go from sideman to solo artist at Chess Records in the manner of his live shows. However, Leonard Chess thought no one would want to hear his "noise." Then, sometime in 1968, he was called into Leonard's office where the label president put Cream's *Wheels of Fire* on a turntable. He then proceeded to bend over his desk and instruct Buddy to "kick me in the ass."

Performance Tip: No one yet has approached the explosive heights and dramatic, dynamic whispers to which he swoops back and forth with striking emotion. But it is worth a try.

Fig. 91

Fig. 95

Lonnie Mack
(1941–2016)

One of the earliest, if not the first blues-rock guitar hero, Lonnie Mack had the credibility and the chops to play the blues authentically and with authority. Indeed, his early session work with legends like James Brown, Freddie King, and others speaks to this. In 1963 at the end of a session with time left over, he was given the opportunity to record something of his own. He opted for his instrumental version of Chuck Berry's "Memphis, Tennessee," and the rest is history. While out on the road, he was notified that it had been released as a single and was racing up the charts. He returned and recorded the blues, rock, and chicken-pickin' classic album *The Wham of That Memphis Man* with instrumentals and vocal numbers. Thus, a solo career of ups and downs was launched.

Performance Tip: Mack played a Gibson Flying V with a Bigsby vibrato arm installed between the wings, and he employed a capo regularly. Both contributed to fast vibrato passages and lightning pull-offs.

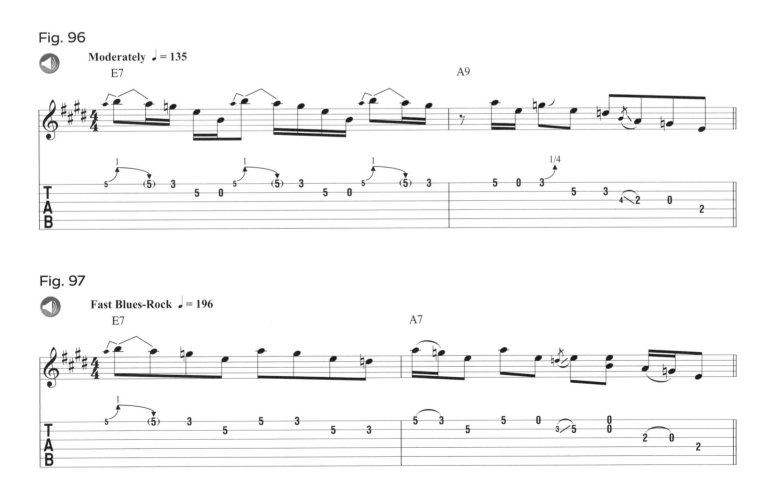

Fig. 96

Fig. 97

Fig. 98

Fig. 99

Fig. 100

Mike Bloomfield
(1943–1981)

Following Lonnie Mack, another guitar hero emerged in the 1960s in the guise of Mike Bloomfield. Though he would dabble in rock, particularly with Bob Dylan, he was an authentic blues guitarist from Chicago where he cut his teeth in the black clubs. Gigs and recordings with Al Kooper, including two *Super Session* albums, not to mention his pioneering playing with the Paul Butterfield Blues Band, sealed his fame. A scholar of the blues and blues guitar, Bloomfield gifted guitarists with the instructional CD *If You Love These Blues, Play 'Em as You Please*.

Performance Tip: Bloomfield would prominently incorporate the ♭5th from the blues scale more often than many of his contemporaries. The bluesy "tang" of it can be heard in Fig. 104 (C♭, or B).

Fig. 101

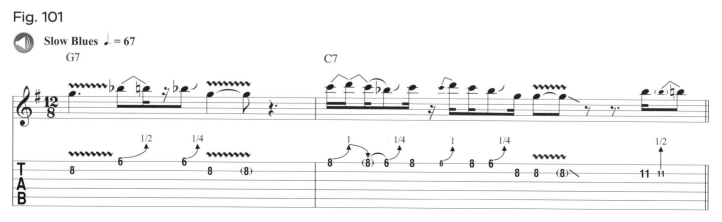

Fig. 102

Slow Blues ♩ = 50

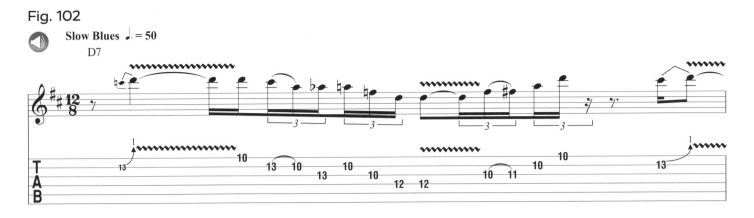

G9

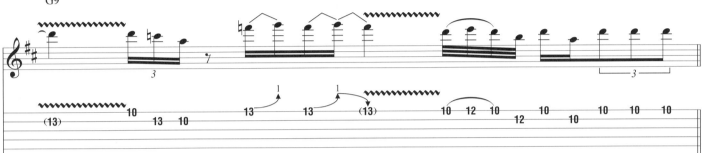

Fig. 103

Latin-Rock ♩ = 129

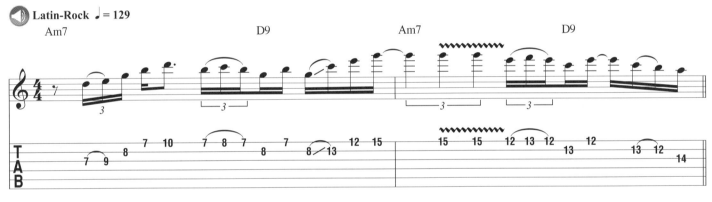

Fig. 104

Slow Blues ♩ = 48

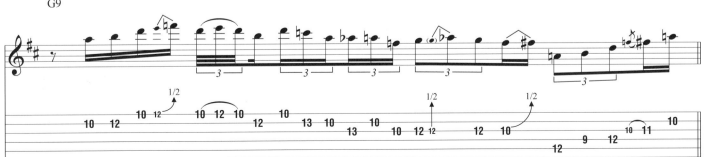

G9

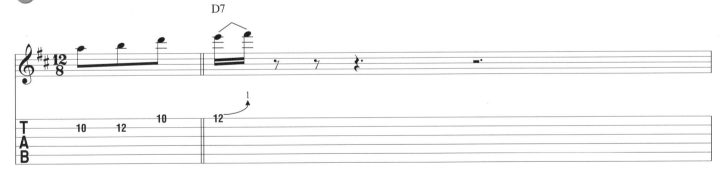

Fig. 105

Eric Clapton
(1945–)

Known at one time in Great Britain as "Slowhand" and "God," Eric Clapton has been a force in blues and rock since the early 1960s. Indeed, his career resume is comprised of veering from rock to blues and back again many times. However, through it all, he has maintained the blues foundation in his playing, based on the legendary artists who inspired him. B.B. King, Albert King, Freddie King, and Otis Rush would head the list with Hubert Sumlin and Buddy Guy also in the mix.

Performance Tip: One of the outstanding characteristics of Clapton's style is his lyrical phrasing involving multiple bends, hammer-ons, and pull-offs composed logically of tension and release.

Fig. 106

Fig. 107

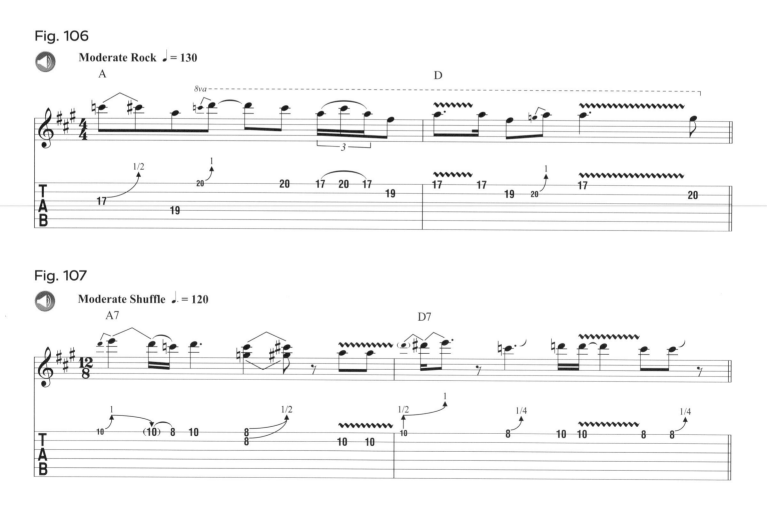

Fig. 108

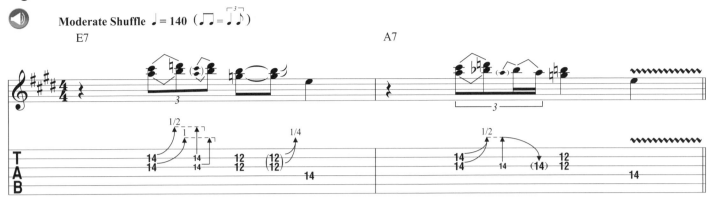

Fig. 109

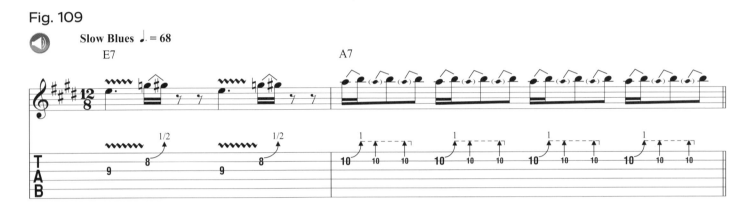

Fig. 110

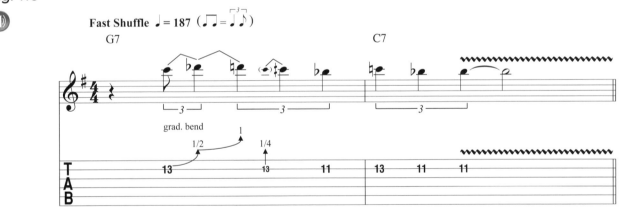

Peter Green
(1946–2020)

Peter Green was famously complimented by B.B. King with the statement, "He was the only guitarist to make me sweat." He made others perspire, too. But mostly, he inspired legions who he thrilled after replacing Eric Clapton in the Bluesbreakers and then with his blues band, Fleetwood Mac, in the late 1960s. His song "The Supernatural," with the former aggregation, represented the shape of things to come with its long, sustained, heavily-reverbed lead lines. "Black Magic Woman" and "Oh, Well" became blues-rock standards. Along the way, he also recorded dozens of authentic 12-bar blues which continued to confirm B.B. King's praise.

Performance Tip: Green was an exceptionally expressive and emotional artist with long, sensuous bends and vibrato. His "cry" had a significant influence on Carlos Santana.

Fig. 111

Slow Blues ♩. = 50

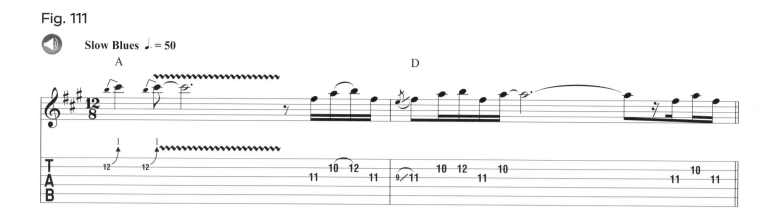

Fig. 112

Moderately fast ♩ = 138

Fig. 113

Moderately ♩ = 100

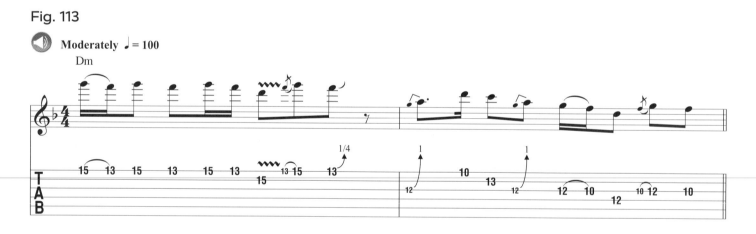

Fig. 114

Slow Blues ♩. = 50

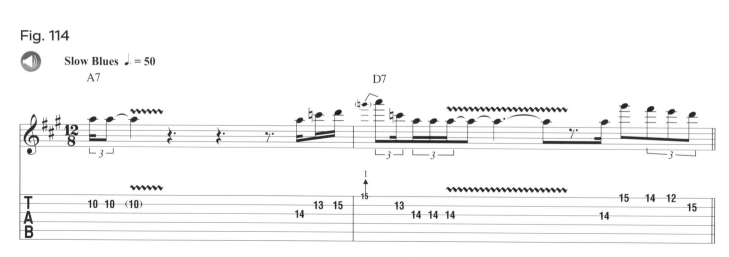

Fig. 115

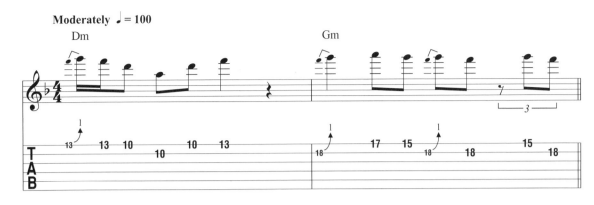

Duane Allman
(1946–1971)

"Skydog" flashed against the firmament like a shooting star. Following session work in the South with Aretha Franklin and Wilson Pickett, in 1968, he was spotted glowing brightly with his Allman Brothers Band and blazed his way into blues-rock immortality. His hiatus from the Brothers in 1970 to join Eric Clapton on "Layla" was a tantalizing preview of a possible future historic pairing of two blues guitar heroes. Tragically, he perished at the too young age of 24 in a motorcycle accident.

Performance Tip: Though rightly lionized as an extraordinary slide guitarist, his fretted lead work combines technical excellence with genuine blues feel. Observe the compressed clusters and repetition of notes which create palpable musical tension and energy.

Fig. 116

Fig. 117

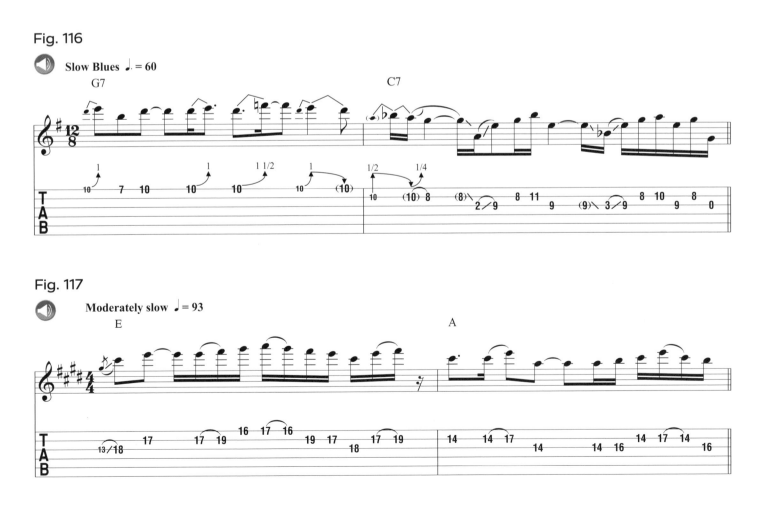

Fig. 118

Slow Blues ♩ = 40

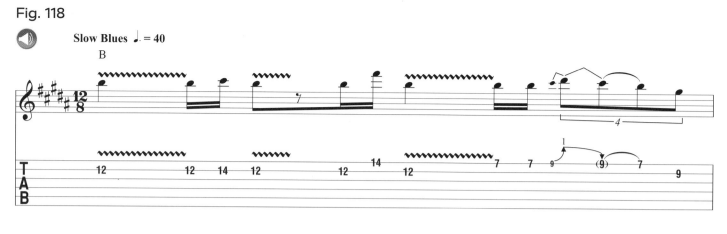

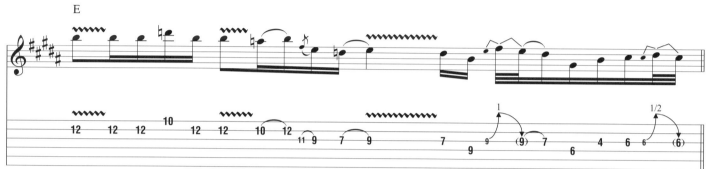

Fig. 119

Slow Blues ♩. = 60

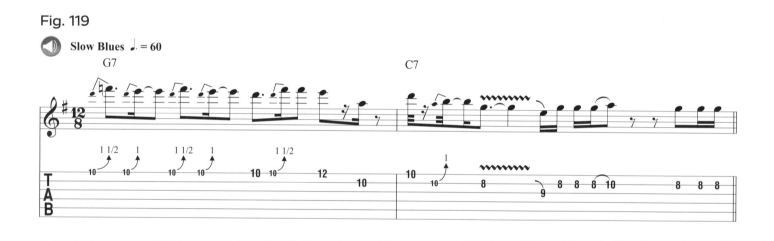

Fig. 120

Moderately fast Shuffle ♩ = 138

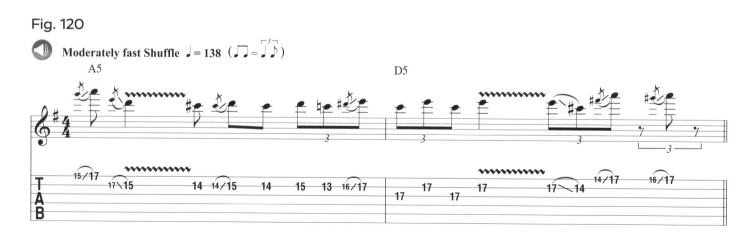

Chapter IV: 1970s

Son Seals
(1942–2004)

Frank "Son" Seals practically inaugurated a second "blues revival" single-handedly with *Son Seals Blues Band* in 1973 and the even more profound *Midnight Son* in 1976. As pertinent or even more so, he was a dynamic, explosive guitarist onstage. His *Live and Burning* from 1978 is a must-have in lieu of going back in time to experience him in person. Likewise, check out his filmed master class *Chicago Blues Guitar*.

Performance Tip: His aggressive approach to pick most notes and the rhythmic accuracy with which they are executed possibly derives from his days as a 13-year old drummer behind Robert Nighthawk.

Fig. 121

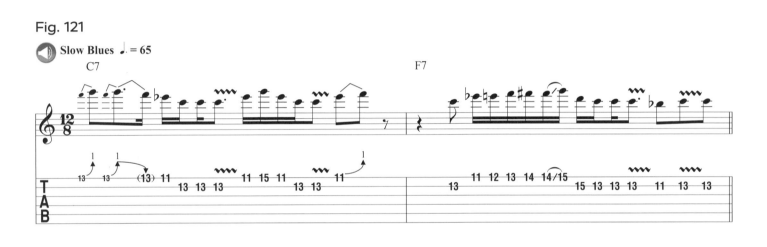

Fig. 122

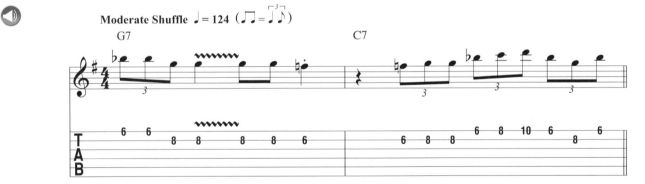

Fig. 123

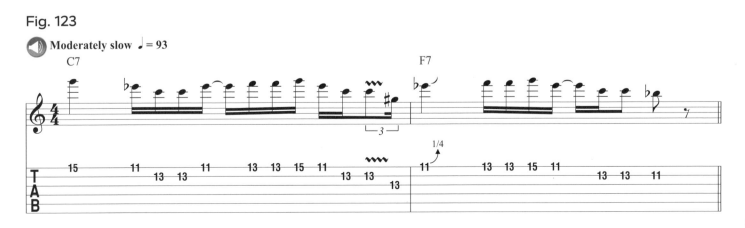

Fig. 124

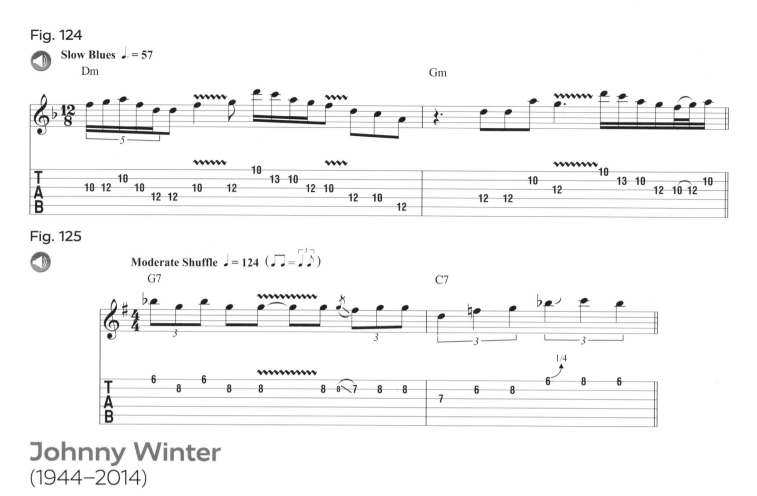

Fig. 125

Johnny Winter
(1944–2014)

Few outside of his home state of Texas had heard of Johnny Winter in the late '60s, save for Mike Bloomfield who had jammed with him previously in Chicago. When "Bloomers" invited the blues phenom to sit in at the Fillmore East in December, 1968, his spectacular version of "It's My Own Fault" convinced the Columbia Records representatives in attendance to ink him to a $600k signing bonus in 1969. A 40-plus year career boasted Winter playing blues and rock with unbridled passion and power. The former showed him to be an authentic conduit for the perpetuation of the music while the latter revealed him an enthusiastic interpreter of classic rock, most notably by the Rolling Stones.

Performance Tip: Like Duane Allman, Winter was particularly adept at slide guitar while being a dynamo when playing straight lead. Similar to B.B. King, he was fond of bending the ♭3rd with his index finger one-quarter step to the true "blue note" in between the ♭3rd and natural 3rd.

Fig. 126

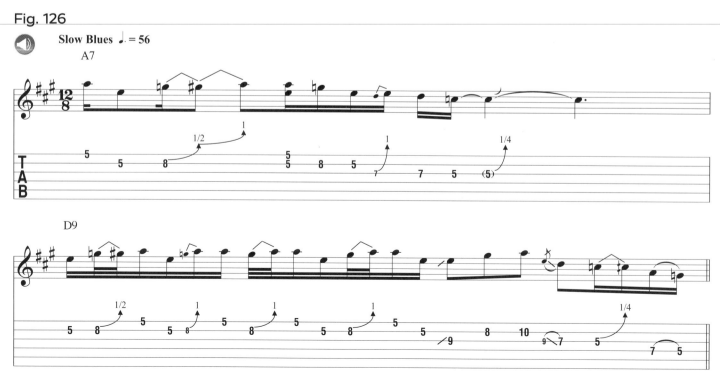

Fig. 127

Fig. 128

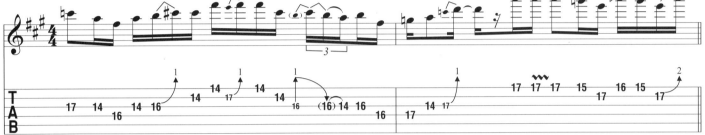

Fig. 129

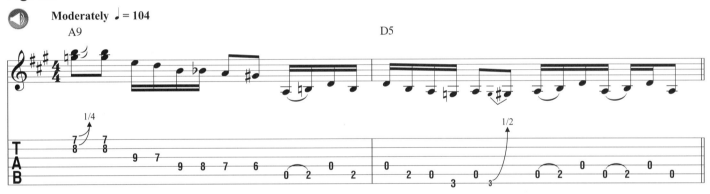

Fig. 130

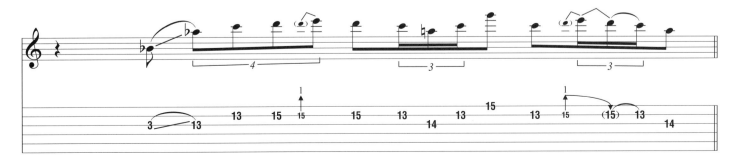

Roy Buchanan
(1939–1988)

Being referred to as "The Best Unknown Guitarist in the World" in a 1971 PBS documentary (actually titled *Introducing Roy Buchanan*) was a mixed blessing. For example, if he was the "best," why had he remained "unknown" for so long? The easy answer is he did not sing very well, if at all, making him a questionable investment for a record label. Another was his personality, which unfortunately deteriorated over time from substance abuse. Nonetheless, he was and remains an unsurpassed blues and rock guitar hero to countless players due to his emotional blues and genre-stretching rock. His tragic death by hanging in a Virginia jail cell was officially termed a suicide, though family and friends deny it.

Performance Tip: His stinging bends, emotional vibrato, and "singing" sustain were produced mainly with his fingers and his soul. That said, a vintage Telecaster and Fender combo amp on his classic early albums enabled his extraordinary ability to squeeze heretofore unheard expressive sounds from that basic solidbody guitar.

Fig. 131

Fig. 132

Fig. 133

Slow Blues ♩ = 70

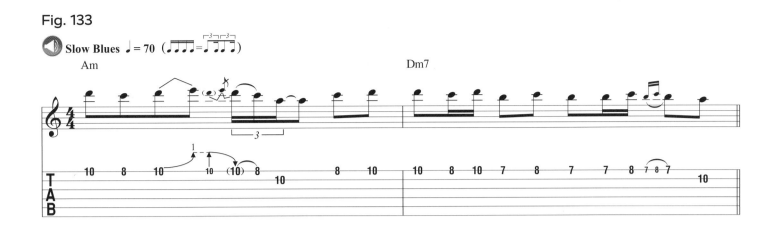

Fig. 134

Moderately fast ♩ = 142

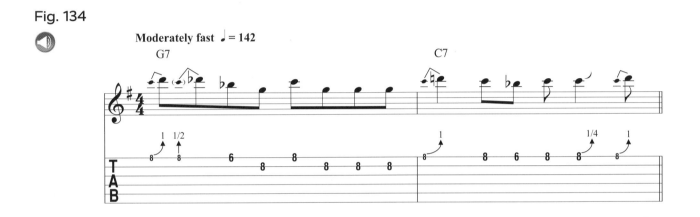

Fig. 135

Slow Blues ♩ = 61

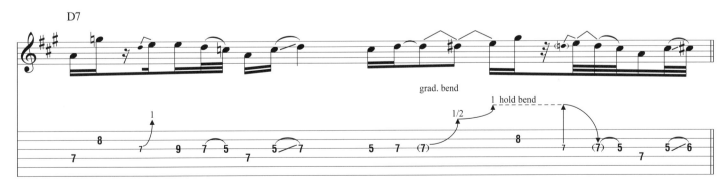

Chapter V: 1980s

Luther Allison
(1939–1997)

Luther Allison took a circuitous path to arrive belatedly at the type of blues superstardom enjoyed by Buddy Guy. In the '50s and '60s, he played in various bands in Chicago, often with his brothers. Freddie King became a mentor, and Allison took over his band when the Texas legend went on the road. He released his first album on Delmark Records in 1969. In 1972, he signed with Motown Records and toured Europe during the '70s. He moved to France in 1977 where he recorded and shuffled back and forth to the States until the early '90s. In 1994, he made the momentous decision to sign with Alligator Records and moved back to the U.S. full time. Tours, awards, and subsequently critically acclaimed albums followed as he was finally able to reap the career spoils he so justly earned.

Performance Tip: Rippling and searing high-register riffs, featuring repetitive notes create scintillating musical tension which cuts like a knife.

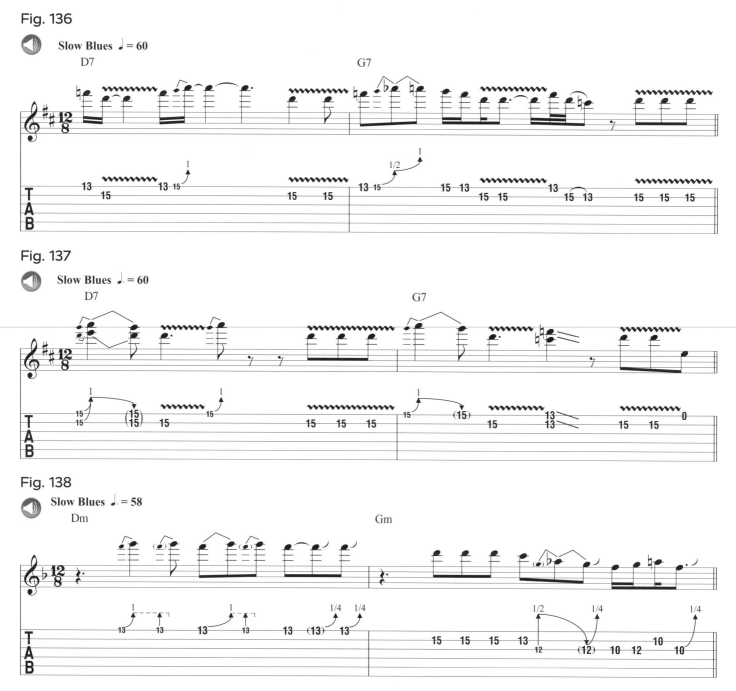

44

Fig. 139

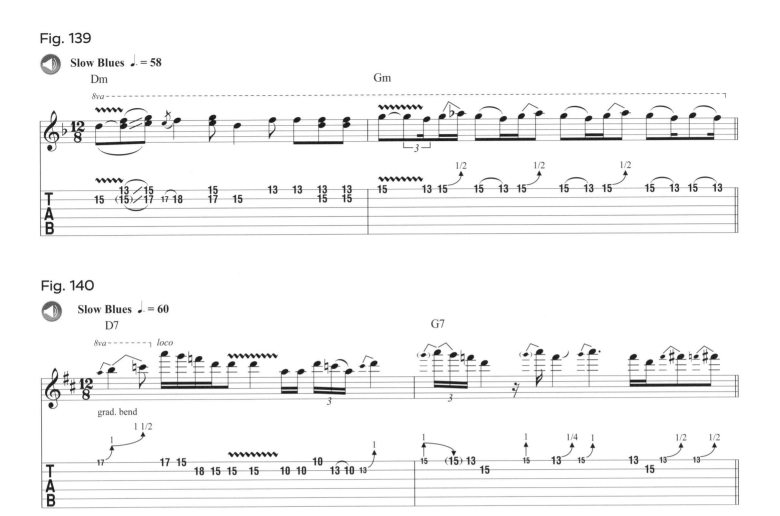

Stevie Ray Vaughan
(1954–1990)

The blues are seemingly self-perpetuating. However, every decade or so since T-Bone Walker "electrified" the music world in the early '40s, a guitarist comes along to "revive" it. In the late '40s and early '50s it was Muddy Waters and John Lee Hooker. In the '60s, it was the British contingent led by Eric Clapton. Son Seals stood out on the Chicago scene in the '70s, and Stevie Ray Vaughan busted out nationally and internationally in the '80s. Influenced significantly by Albert King, Buddy Guy, and Lonnie Mack, along with Jimi Hendrix, he embodied the power and commitment of his forebearers while ramping the energy quotient up exponentially. Then, like the earlier blues guitar hero Duane Allman, he came to the untimeliest of ends, tragically dying in a helicopter crash after a performance in Wisconsin. Though other pretenders to the blues guitar throne have come and gone, his legacy lives on undiminished.

Performance Tip: Stevie Ray Vaughan had spectacular chops and was unafraid to use them. Nonetheless, he was cognizant of the chord changes and consistently acknowledged them, be it with a note, scale riff, or chordal form.

Fig. 141

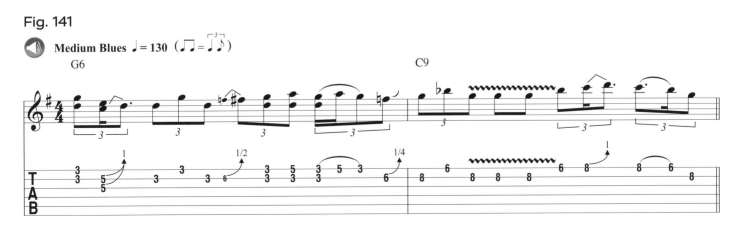

Robert Cray
(1953–)

Though as much or more an R&B and soul music guitarist, the blues of Robert Cray are as stone authentic as anyone. Inspired by seeing Albert Collins, Freddie King, and Muddy Waters in concert, at the age of 20 he formed a band in Eugene, Oregon. His first album, *Who's Been Talkin'* in 1980 contained the most straight-ahead blues until *Showdown!* with Texas blues legends Albert Collins and Johnny Copeland. In between were two original soul blues albums, followed by his breakthrough commercial success *Strong Persuader* in 1986. An in-demand sideman, he has recorded with John Lee Hooker, Chuck Berry, Tina Turner, and B.B. King, among others. In August 1990, Cray appeared with Eric Clapton, Buddy Guy, Jimmie Vaughan, and Stevie Ray Vaughan at a show in Wisconsin, the same one after which Vaughan perished.

Performance Tip: Cray is nothing if not tasty with choice "target" notes navigating the chord changes and undulating phrasing punctuated by slinky bends.

Fig. 149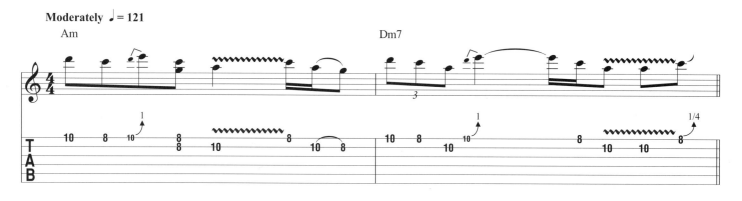

Fig. 150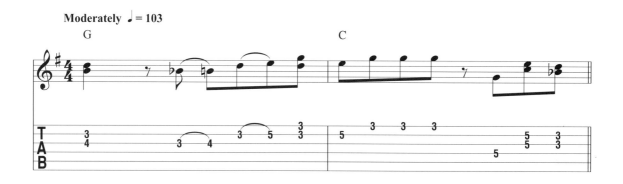